# It Begins with an A

# It Begins with an A

## Stephanie Calmenson

## Illustrated by Marisabina Russo

Hyperion Books for Children

New York

You travel in this.    It begins with an A.

It starts on the ground,    then flies up, up, away!

W H A T    I S    I T

This red rubber toy    begins with a *B*.

It's round. It bounces.    You throw it to me.

W  H  A  T        I  S    I  T  ?

This takes your picture.

It starts with a C.

Get ready, get set.

Now smile for me!

W H A T        I S   I T ?

It's the toy I hug and talk to.

Its name begins with *D*.

With orange hair and button eyes,

it looks a lot like me.

W H A T     I S     I T ?

This comes from a hen.

It starts with an *E*.

I ate one for breakfast.

Dad cooked it for me.

W H A T    I S    I T ?

It's the part of your body    you put into your shoe.

It starts with an *F*,    and we each have two.

W  H  A  T    I  S    I  T  ?

She's a long-necked animal.

Her name starts with G.

She stretches up high

to eat leaves from a tree.

WHAT IS SHE?

For banging in nails,

I always will choose it.

It begins with *H*.

Oh, what noise when I use it!

W H A T   I S   I T ?

You spread this on cake.

It is something you eat.

It begins with an *l*.

Taste it—it's sweet!

W H A T     I S     I T ?

It's a place to keep things.

The first letter is *J*.

It's where peanut butter,

cookies, or pickles can stay.

W  H  A  T          I  S      I  T  ?

She jumps, jumps, jumps!

Her name starts with *K*.

She has a pocket in front

where her baby can stay.

W H A T   I S   S H E ?

This is a candy   that comes on a stick.

It starts with an *L*,   and it's fun to lick.

W H A T     I S     I T ?

It's up in the sky    with the stars, shining bright.

The first letter is M,    and it lights up the night.

W    H    A    T        I    S        I    T    ?

This starts with an N.

You know it quite well.

It's right on your face.

You use it to smell.

**W H A T     I S     I T ?**

Hoot! Hoot! Hoot!   I wonder if you know

this night bird's name.   It begins with an O.

W H A T   I S   I T ?

It starts with a *P.*

I have one on my bed.

When I go to sleep at night,

it's where I rest my head.

W H A T      I S      I T ?

Here is a coin      that begins with a *Q*.

For twenty-five pennies,      I'll give one to you.

W H A T      I S   I T ?

Long ears, cotton tail,

his name begins with *R*.

For a tasty, crunchy carrot,

this animal will hop far.

W H A T     I S     H E ?

This food starts with S.

It's long and it's thin.

I eat it with tomato sauce

that drips down to my chin.

W H A T        I S    I T ?

A squirrel has a bushy one.

It starts with a *T*.

My dog has a happy one.

She wags it for me.

W H A T     I S   I T ?

It starts with a *U*.    I have one that's red.

I stay dry in the rain    when it's over my head.

W H A T        I S    I T ?

It's shaped like a heart.

The first letter is *V*.

It says, "I love you,

and I hope you love me."

**W H A T   I S   I T ?**

This starts with a *W*.

I like it! It's wet!

I splash in a tub of it.

Look how clean I can get!

**W H A T     I S     I T ?**

The first letter is an X.

It's a picture of me.

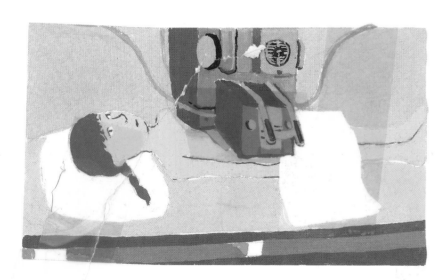

It shows all my bones

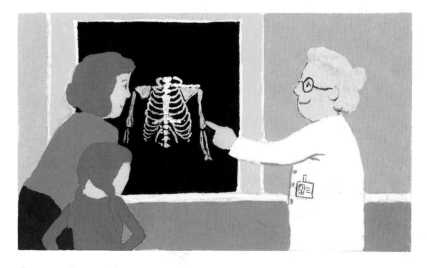

for the doctor to see.

WHAT IS IT?

This begins with a Y.

It's a toy on a string.

It goes down and up.

It's a spinning thing!

W H A T   I S   I T ?

This animal's name    begins with a Z.

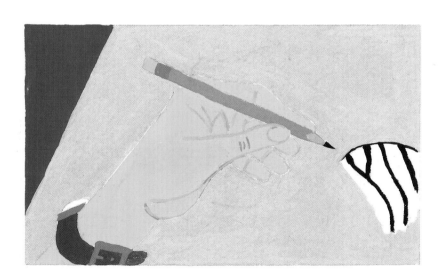

She looks like a pretty    striped pony to me.

W  H  A  T    I  S    S  H  E  ?

**A** Airplane

**B** Ball

**C** Camera

**D** Doll

**E** Egg

**F** Foot

**G** Giraffe

**H** Hammer

**I** Icing

**J** Jar

**K** Kangaroo

**L** Lollypop

**M** Moon

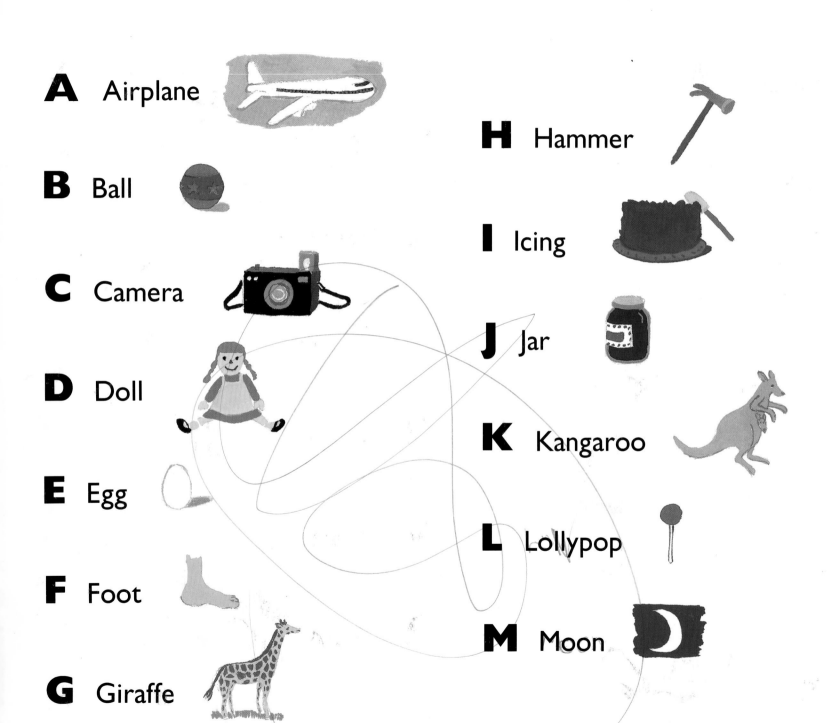

**N** Nose

**O** Owl

**P** Pillow

**Q** Quarter

**R** Rabbit

**S** Spaghetti

**T** Tail

**U** Umbrella

**V** Valentine

**W** Water

**X** X ray

**Y** Yo-yo

**Z** Zebra

To Sara Dager
—S. C.

For William and Christopher
—M. R.

For information address Hyperion Books for Children,
114 Fifth Avenue, New York, New York 10011.

FIRST EDITION
1  3  5  7  9  10  8  6  4  2

Library of Congress Cataloging-in-Publication Data
Calmenson, Stephanie.
It begins with an A / Stephanie Calmenson;
illustrated by Marisabina Russo.—1st ed.   p.   cm.
Summary: Rhyming riddles challenge the reader
to guess objects beginning with letters A to Z.
ISBN 1-56282-122-9 (trade)—ISBN 1-56282-123-7 (lib. bdg.)
1. Riddles, Juvenile.    2. Alphabet rhymes.
[1. Riddles.    2. Alphabet.]
I. Russo, Marisabina, ill.    II. Title.
PN6371.5.C324  1993
818'.5402—dc20    [E]
92-72016  CIP  AC

The artwork for each picture is prepared using gouache.
This book is set in 22-point Gill Sans.
Book design by Joann Hill Lovinski.